Claude Monet

The Clouds, the Water

by Jacqueline and Maurice Guillaud

Guillaud Miniatures

Clarkson N. Potter, Inc./New York
Guillaud Editions Paris-New York

Claude Monet was born in Paris in 1840 to parents who were natives of the capital. When he was five, the family moved to Le Havre where, at the age of fifteen, he first attracted the attention of Eugene Boudin with caricatures exhibited in the window of a local bookshop. Returning to Paris in 1857, he enrolled at the Academie Suisse and made the acquaintance of Pissarro.

After military service in Algeria, he studied at the Gleyre studio, where he became friends with Renoir and Sisley. However, he found the academic environment stifling and, in an effort to break free of what he considered sterile conventions, looking to the work of Turner, he went to the forest of Fontainebleau and began to work from nature. In Normandy, between 1864 and 1868, he painted *Picnic, Terrace in Le Havre, Women in the Garden*, and followed with a number of landscapes painted in Trouville, Fecamp, and Etretat.

Although his talent was recognized by some of the critics, Monet's pictures were rejected by the Salons. In his luminous landscapes of Bougival and Argenteuil he emphasized the primacy of light by using color in a new way, laying pure paint on the canvas without mixing it on the palette.

At the outbreak of the Franco-Prussian War in 1870, he went to London, where he was joined by Pissarro and Sisley. There he was introduced to Durand-Ruel, who later became the three artists' dealer. After a brief stay in Holland, Monet returned to Argenteuil on the Seine, where he lived in a houseboat converted into a studio.

As the official Salons continued to show no interest in the work of the ex-pupils of the Gleyre studio, and the three friends had difficulty in finding buyers, they decided to promote themselves by founding *the Société Anonyme des Peintres, Sculpteurs et Graveurs* ("Painters, Sculptors, and Engravers, Inc."). In 1874 they staged an exhibition, at which Monet showed his *Impression, Rising Sun*. Impressed by this painting, Louis Leroy spoke of the "exhibition of the Impressionists" in a review published in *Le Charivari*.

He stated that these artists sought to capture the light of a brief instant, arresting the flux of time in relation to the scene depicted; they gave priority to the personal impression rather than the objective depiction of the subject; they preferred to work outdoors, regardless of the weather, adding the finishing touches in the studio; and they strove to exact the utmost from the sensation of color.

Monet participated in further group exhibitions, showing eighteen canvases in 1876, thirty in 1877, and twenty nine - most of them painted at Vetheuil - in 1879.

He soon grew bored with the lack of new motifs offered by Poissy, where he had moved in 1881, and, wishing to provide a home for Alice Hoschede (who became his wife on July 16, 1892), her six, and his own two children, he took a house in Giverny in the Eure region, forty four miles from Paris, in 1883.

Collectors and dealers were now taking an interest in Monet's work. He began to go off on "painting trips", which took him to Antibes, Menton, Bordighera, Genova, and later to Spain, where he visited the Prado and Toledo.

In Antibes, in 1888, he painted his first "series": the same subject observed at different times of day. In 1892 he painted the facade of Rouen Cathedral forty times, under varying effects of light. "Imagine, I get up before six and am at work from seven to half-past six in the evening, standing the whole time, nine canvases... I had a succession of nightmares last night: the cathedral was bearing down on me, it looked blue, then pink, then yellow."

Though residing some distance from Paris, Monet often went to the capital to attend concerts or the theater. He dined with his friends - painters, critics, writers, musicians and actors, including Mirbeau, Mallarme, Valery, Clemenceau, and the Guitrys.

The death of his wife on May 19, 1911, cast a shadow over the final years of his life, and he was also troubled by failing eyesight. Nevertheless, he continued to pursue his "project" to the utmost. Narrative became pure poetry, the moment became music, the material: Abstraction. The artist's endeavor was no longer to capture the fleeting moment of the subject, but that of the painter; his instant in time, experienced in the act of painting. He lived in seclusion in Giverny, with his stepdaughter and daughter-in-law Blanche. There he had a large studio built, twelve by twenty three meters, so that he could paint wall-panels of the *Water-Lilies*. These vast compositions, donated to the state in 1923, were installed in the Orangerie des Tuileries shortly after Monet's death in Giverny on December 6, 1926.

...As for translating the blue of the sea and the sky, it is impossible....this place is drenched in light.... Everything is "gorge-de-pigeon" and "flamme de punch". It is wonderful...

...the Creuse goes down quite perceptibly and when it does so, its waters take on another colour which makes everything look different. In short, where the

water would run in green torrents, we can now see the bottom which is all brown...The Creuse is swelling again and is once more turning yellow...

Branch of the Seine near Giverny II, 1897
Boston, Museum of Fine Arts (bequest of Mrs Walter Scott Fitz)

Ventimiglia, 1884
Glasgow Art Gallery and Museum

Palm Trees at Bordighera, 1884
Metropolitan Museum of Art, (bequest of Miss Adelaïde Milton de Groot)

...I have often told of how one day I found Monet in front of a field of poppies, with four easels, to which by turns, he would give lively strokes as the light shifted in the path of the sun... They would load wheelbarrows, and sometimes small farm vehicles, with a pile of utensils, in order to set up a series of outdoor studios. The easels would be lined up on the grass, ready for combat between Monet and the sun...G.C.

Port-Goulphar, 1887
Sydney, Art Gallery of New South Wales

Rocks at Belle-Ile, 1886
Reims, Musée Saint-Denis

The Creuse Valley, 1889
Colmar, Musée d'Unterlinden

Les Eaux Semblantes, Dark Weather, 1889
Wuppertal Elberfeld, Von der Heydt, Museum der Stadt

Poplars on the Bank of the Epte River, 1891
Edinburgh, The National Gallery of Scotland

Poplars, Three Pink Trees, Autumn, 1891
Philadelphia Museum of Art (bequest of Chester Dale)

Field of Irises at Giverny, 1887
Paris, Musée Marmottan

Field of Poppies, 1890
Northampton, Smith College Museum of Art

Haystack at Sunset near Giverny, 1891
Boston, Museum of Fine Arts (Juliana Cheney Edwards Collection)

Vetheuil in the Morning, 1901
Lille, Musée des Beaux-Arts

Venice, the Doge Palace, 1908
Switzerland, Private Collection

Branch of the Seine near Giverny, 1897
Paris, Musée d'Orsay

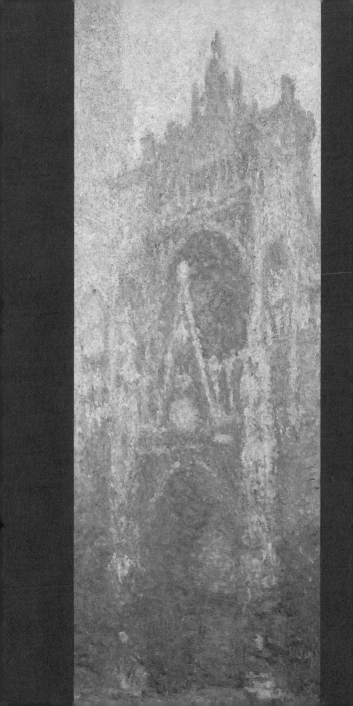

The Gate and the Albane Tower at Dawn, 1894
Boston, Museum of Fine Arts (Tompkins Collection)

...When looking closely at these cathedrals of Monet's, they seem to be made of I don't know what kind of multicoloured mortar, crushed onto the canvas in a fit of rage. All this wild transport comes doubtless from passion. But from science as well. How can an artist, only a few centimeters away from his canvas, realize both the exact and subtle effects that can only be appreciated at a distance? This is the disconcerting mystery of his retinal screen. G.C.

The Gate, 1894
Weimar, Schlossmuseum

Rouen Cathedral in the Sun, 1894
Boston, Museum of Fine Arts (Juliana Cheney Edwards Collection)

Rouen Cathedral, Gate and the Albane Tower, in the Morning, 1894
Basil, Galerie Beyeler

London, the Parliament, Clearing in the Fog, 1904
Paris, Musée d'Orsay

London, the Parliament, 1905
Paris, Musée Marmottan

Watergarden and Clouds, 1903
U.S.A., Private Collection

Waterlilies and Pond, 1905
Cardiff, National Museum of Wales

The Waterlily Pond, Green Harmony, 1899
Paris, Musée d'Orsay

Waterlilies, Water Landscape, 1903
Tokyo, Bridgestone Museum of Art, Ishibashi Foundation

Waterlilies and Pond, 1908
Cardiff, National Museum of Wales

The panels of *Nymphéas*
show him to us as madly
striving to realize the
impossible. Out of his
trembling hand shoots
rockets of luminescence
that make new blazes of
light flash through a full
brush... G.C.

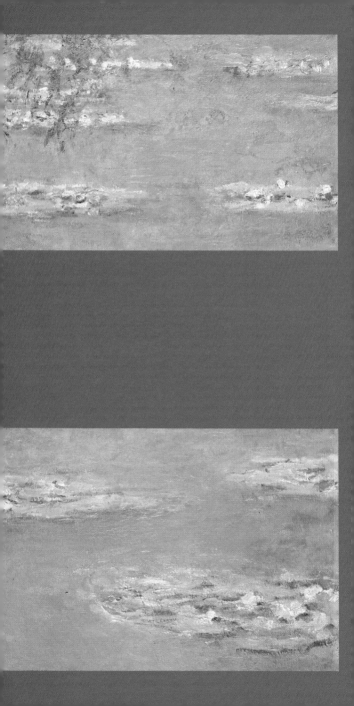

Waterlilies, 1907
Houston, Museum of Fine Arts (bequest of Mrs Harry C. Hanszen)

Waterlilies, 1908
Dallas Museum of Art (bequest of the Meadows Foundation)

Clouds, 1914/18
Paris, Musée de l'Orangerie

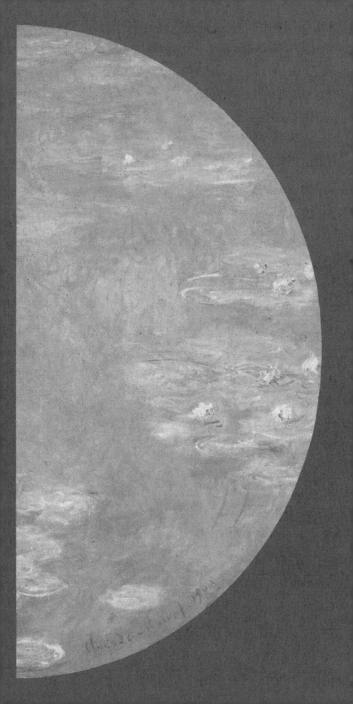

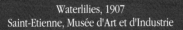

Waterlilies, 1907
Saint-Etienne, Musée d'Art et d'Industrie

...Regarding the colors I use, is it as interesting as all that ? I do not think so, given that one might produce better and more luminous colors from an entirely different palette. The real point is to know how to use colors, the choice of which is basically no more than a question of habit.

I use the following:

lead white

cadmium yellow

vermilion

dark madder

cobalt blue

emerald green, and that is all.

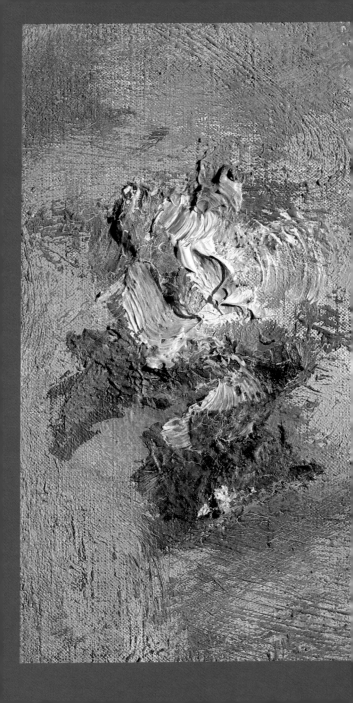

I am enraptured, Giverny is the ideal country for me...

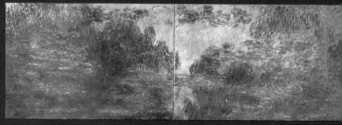

Waterlilies, c. 1914/22
Zurich, Kunsthaus

Waterlilies at Twilight, c. 1916/1922
Zurich, Kunsthaus

The Willow, 1920
Paris, Musée Marmottan

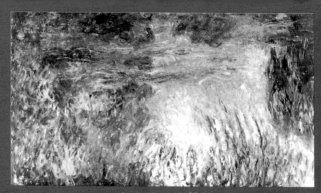

Setting Sun, 1914/18
Paris, Musée de l'Orangerie

The Garden at Giverny, 1902
Vienna, Kunsthistorisches Museum

The Weeping Willow, 1922
Basil, Galerie Beyeler

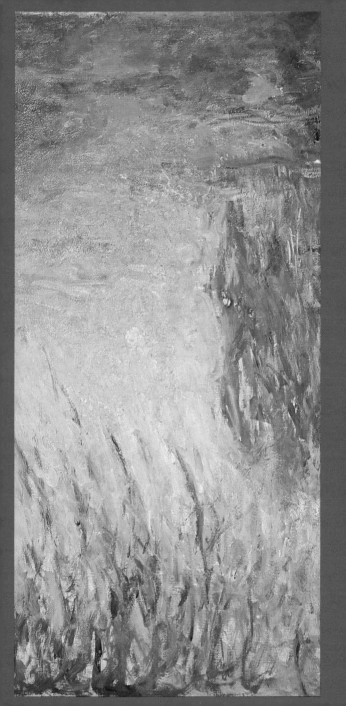

The Rose Bush Lane at Giverny, 1918
Paris, Musée Marmottan

Waterlilies: Japanese Footbridge, c. 1922
Minneapolis Institute of Arts

Waterlilies, Evening, 1907
Paris, Musée Marmottan

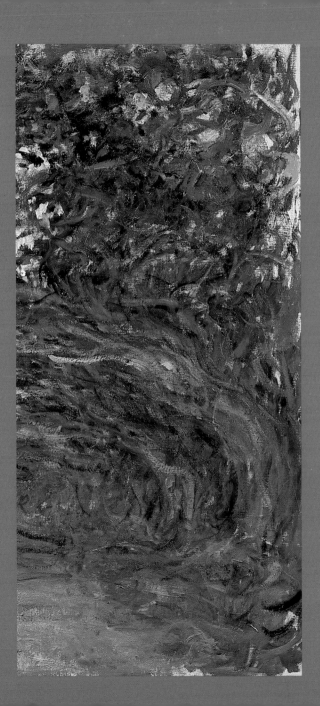

The 42 paintings which are reproduced here were all created during Monet's Giverny period (1883-1926)

Branch of the Seine near Giverny II (two details on front and back of cover); *Ventimiglia* (two details); *Palm Trees at Bordighera* (four details); *Port-Goulphar* (two details); *Rocks at Belle-Ile* (two details); *The Creuse Valley* (two details); *Les Eaux Semblantes, Dark Weather* (two details); *Branch of the Seine near Giverny II* (87 x 98); *Ventimiglia* (65 x 91.7); *Autumn* (92 x 73); *Field of Irises at Giverny* (45 x 100); *Field of Poppies* (60.3 x 100.7) *Haystack at Sunset near Giverny* (73 x 92); *Vetheuil in the Morning* (89 x 92); *Venice, the Doge Palace* (90 x 124); *Branch of the Seine near Giverny* (75 x 92.5, two details); *The Gate and the Albane Tower at Dawn* (two details); *The Rouen Cathedral in the Sun* (two details); *The Gate* (detail); *The Rouen Cathedral, Gate and the Albane Tower in the Morning* (two details) ; *London, the Parliament Clearing in the Fog* (two details) ;

Waterlilies and Agapantas, 1922
Paris, Musée Marmottan

Palm Trees at Bordighera (65 x 81); *Poplars on the Bank of the Epte River* (three details); *Poplars, Three Pink Trees, Autumn* (two details); *Field of Irises at Giverny* (two details); *Field of Poppies* (two details); *Port-Goulphar* (81 x 65); *Rocks at Belle-Ile* (65 x 81); *The Creuse Valley* (73 x 70); *Haystack at Sunset near Giverny* (detail); *Vetheuil in the Morning* (two details); *Venice, the Doge Palace* (detail); *Les Eaux Semblantes, Dark Weather* (73 x 92); *Poplars on the Bank of the Epte River* (81.5 x 82); *Poplars, Three Pink Trees, Autumn* (92 x 73); *Field of Irises at Giverny* (45 x 100); *Field of Poppies* (60.3 x 100.7) *The Gate and the Albane Tower at Dawn* (106 x 74); *The Rouen Cathedral in the Sun* (100 x 65); *The Gate* (100 x 65); *London, the Parliament* (six details); *Watergarden and Clouds* (six details); 1905 *Waterlilies, Waterlandscape,* (six details); *The Rouen Cathedral, Gate and the Albane Tower in the Morning* (106.5 x 73.5); *London, the Parliament Clearing in the Fog* (81 x 92); *London, the Parliament* (81 x 92); *Watergarden and Clouds* (62 x 107); *Waterlilies and Pond*, 1905 (79 x 96.5); *The*

Waterlily Pond, Green Harmony (89 x 93); *Waterlilies, Waterlandscape*, 1903 (81 x 99); *Waterlilies and Pond*, 1908 (96.5 x 79); *The Waterlily Pond, Green Harmony* (detail); *Waterlilies, Waterlandscape*, 1903 (three details); *Waterlilies and Pond, 1908* (detail); *Waterlilies*, 1907 (92 x 81); *Waterlilies*, (round, 80 cm diameter); *Clouds*, 1914/18 (197 x 1275, three panels, room 1); *Waterlilies*, 1907 (two details); *Waterlilies*, 1908 (two details); *Clouds*, 1914/18 (two details); *Waterlilies*, 1907 (round, 80 cm diameter, two details); *Waterlilies* (two details); *Waterlilies at Twilight* (two details); *Waterlilies* (78.75 x 236.25); *Waterlilies at Twilight* (200 x 600); *Willow* (200 x 180, detail); *Setting Sun* (197 x 600, one panel, room1); *The Garden at Giverny*, 1902 (89 x 92); *Weeping Willow* (120.5 x 100); *Setting Sun* (detail); *The Rose Tree Lane at Giverny* (92 x 89); *Waterlilies: Japanese Footbridge* (89.2 x 116.2) *Waterlilies, Evening* (100 x 73); *The Garden at Giverny*, 1902 (detail); *Weeping Willow* (two details); *The Rose Tree Lane at Giverny* (detail); *Waterlilies: Japanese Footbridge* (two details); *Waterlilies, Evening* (two details); *Waterlilies and Agapantas* (140 x 120, two details); *Wysteria* (two details, 100 x 200); *The Garden, Giverny*, 1917 (117 x 83, two details).

All measurements are in centi-meters.

All text in italics are Claude Monet's G. C.: Georges Clémenceau in *Claude Monet: Cinquante ans d'amitié*, Paris 1928

Claude Monet: Les Nymphéas, Paris 1928

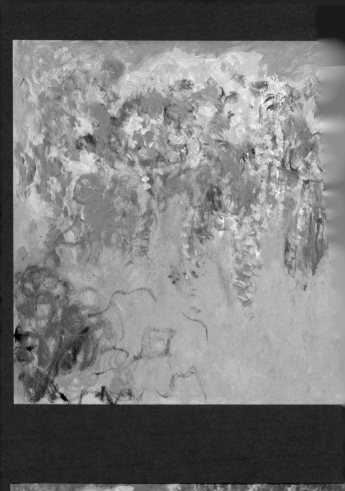

Wysteria, c. 1920
Dreux, Musée d'Art et d'Histoire Marcel Dessal

The Garden, Giverny, 1917
Grenoble, Musée de Peinture et de Sculpture

Texts and design by Maurice Guillaud ©

The works of Claude Monet © Spadem
© 1989 Jacqueline and Maurice Guillaud

Library of Congress Cataloging-in-Publication Data
Guillaud, Jacqueline and Maurice
Claude Monet, the clouds, the water.
1. Monet, Claude, 1840-1926. I. Monet, Claude,
1840-1926. II. Guillaud, Maurice. III. Title.
ND553. M7A4 1989 759.4 88-32389
ISBN 0-517-573059
Published by Clarkson N. Potter Inc.,
225 Park Avenue South
New York NY 10003
Represented in Canada by the Canadian
MANDA Group
Published in France by Guillaud Editions
70 rue René Boulanger 75010 Paris
Printed by Stocchiero Vicenza
Bound by S.P.B.R. France.
Photolitho: Litho Service Verona